LANDSAT 5 SATELLITE IMAGE, MARCH 13, 1987

Clear, non-turbid water
Sediment-laden, turbid water
Wetlands
Bare soils of agricultural fields
Green Vegetation

N

North Edisto River

Bear Island

Ashepoo River

South Edisto River

Edisto Island

Combahee River

Coosaw River

Atlantic Ocean

Broad River

SOUTH CAROLINA'S
ACE BASIN

Fripp Island

SOUTH CAROLINA'S
WETLAND WILDERNESS

THE ACE BASIN

PHOTOGRAPHS AND TEXT BY TOM BLAGDEN, JR.

SPONSORED BY THE NATURE CONSERVANCY OF SOUTH CAROLINA
IN ASSOCIATION WITH FUJI PHOTO FILM, INC.

WESTCLIFFE PUBLISHERS, INC. ENGLEWOOD, COLORADO

ACKNOWLEDGMENTS

Dedicated to Lynn and Sarah, my wife and daughter.

The acknowledgments are located at the beginning of this book for a very important reason: *South Carolina's Wetland Wilderness: The ACE Basin* would not have been possible without assistance and funding from numerous organizations and individuals. This book is symbolic of the ACE Basin protection plan, evolving from individual inspiration to coordinated efforts of many who believe in the importance of the ACE Basin and in photography as the most expressive means of conveying the spirit of this remarkable ecosystem.

To the following organizations and individuals I am deeply grateful: Principally, Westcliffe Publishers and its president, John Fielder, for their environmental commitment to producing a quality book on the ACE Basin despite market risks stemming from the area's relative lack of recognition; Fuji Photo Film, Inc., for their generous financial support, for practicing their homeland tradition of environmental philanthropy in South Carolina, and for encouraging the medium of photography as a powerful environmental tool.

Special thanks to Akira Kumai, president, and Craig White, director of human resources of Fuji Photo Film, Inc.; The Nature Conservancy of South Carolina for co-sponsoring this book and for their role in the conservation of the ACE Basin, and to board member Frank Wideman and Pat Morgan, executive director.

Extra funding was essential to my work through more than two years of photography and preparation. My appreciation goes to Ducks Unlimited Foundation for providing assistance in the solicitation of these funds. For their generosity, I thank The Plumsock Fund, Ethel Jane Bunting, John Henry Dick, Gaylord and Dorothy Donnelley, Winthrop M. Crane, Esther and James Ferguson, Thomas and Martha Blagden, J. Miles Barkley. This project is also funded in part by the South Carolina Arts Commission, which receives support from the National Endowment for the Arts.

I also thank Fuji Photo Film, Inc., and Thomas Shay for providing the film and Bill Prudner, Fuji professional products.

My gratitude goes to the following organizations: The Nature Conservancy, Ducks Unlimited Foundation/Wetlands America Trust, South Carolina Wildlife and Marine Resources Department, U.S. Fish and Wildlife Service, and South Carolina Water Resources Commission.

Many friends and associates helped in all phases of this book. Special thanks to David Soliday, who shared his cabin and hospitality. And thanks, above all, to the many private landowners who gave me the privilege of photographing their properties. I also wish to express my indebtedness to the following people: Gaylord and Dorothy Donnelley; David and Louise Maybank; Dr. Luke Erwin, Jr., and Jennifer and Luke Erwin III; Allen and Dodie Spaulding; David H. Maybank; Peggy Pepper; Hugh Lane, Sr., and Family; Tony Merck; Richard Stuhr; Luke Platt; Mike Prevost; Coy Johnston; Ann Simpson; Tom and Sally Murphy; Bobby Ellis; Richard Porcher; Will Post; Terry Richardson; Donny Browning; Bill Carter; Bill and Sally Whitner; Chester DePratter; Porky and Delores Rhoades; Don Oliver; Ross Catterton; John Hiers; Lew Crouch; Greg Hudson; Joe Hamilton; Steve Kerchner; Ben Ferguson; Tom Bowen; Bill Baldwin; Pat Robinson; John Meffert; Patricia Kusmierski; Ann Starck; Michael Limehouse; Barry Beasley; Linda Lundquist; Greg Koeln; Doug Muchoney and Tim Steele.

Finally, my heartfelt thanks to my wife, Lynn. Through a difficult time, which included the wonderful but consuming demands of parenting our new daughter, Sarah, Lynn cheerfully endured my erratic schedule and moods. She also helped me appreciate the realization that the welfare of the ACE Basin and my sense of home and family are bound to each other — charting our future.

T.B.

International Standard Book Number: 0-929969-71-5
Library of Congress Catalogue Card Number:
    91-066706
Copyright, 1992: Tom Blagden, Jr.
Editor: John Fielder
Assistant Editor: Margaret Terrell Morse
Production Manager: Mary Jo Lawrence
Typographer: Ruth Koning
ACE Basin Satellite Image: Data provided by The Nature
    Conservancy; Image provided by Ducks Unlimited
All quotations from *The Carolina Low-Country,*
    New York: MacMillan Company, 1931.
Printed in Singapore by Tien Wah Press (Pte.), Ltd.
Published by Westcliffe Publishers, Inc.
    2650 South Zuni Street
    Englewood, Colorado 80110

First frontispiece: Sea oats on beachfront dunes, Otter Island
Second frontispiece: Tidal creek at sunset, Otter Island
Third frontispiece: Bald cypress trees, Calfpen Swamp
Title page: Freshwater marsh pond and forest,
    Mary's Island Reserve
Opposite: Chinese tallow in autumn, Jehossee Island,
    Edisto River

Black skimmers, Deveaux Bank   *Opposite: Lowtide oyster beds and mud flats at sunset, behind Hunting Island*

CONTENTS

FOREWORD

The South Carolina Lowcountry is a place where waters — fresh and salt — conspire with the land to create a swampy Eden. It is like no other. Here soft winds whisper through the Spanish moss. Waterfowl and wading birds occur in profusion. Eagles soar, and nature's bounty has been kind to people.

By and large, the impression of people has been light upon the land, but the pressures are clearly mounting. Development, which so often ends up destroying what attracted it in the first place, almost inevitably will bring increasing pressure to bear.

In a sense this is but a small part of the story of misuse and destruction of wetlands. All too often wetlands have been seen to have little practical use, and have been drained, filled or used as dumping grounds. Wetlands were wasteland, and it was but "common sense" to convert them to something else. When I was a child no one put into perspective my admiration for the Dutch for claiming land from the sea by pointing out how this must have undercut North Sea fishery productivity. Today approximately half of all United States wetlands have already been destroyed.

Toward the end of the Carter administration I was requested to help technically with a proposed executive order intended to protect resources of international importance. I initiated some discussion about putting wetlands on the list, but it didn't get very far. I thought about it overnight and called in the next day to say that wetlands were not only so important we should protect all of them, but we should also be trying to create more. Nothing came of that nor of the proposed executive order, and indeed today there still is a struggle between the old wasteland/obstacle to development attitude and the recognition of wetlands as precious resources.

It is remarkable through all of this that the ACE Basin — where the Ashepoo, the Combahee and the Edisto flow into a common embayment — continues to be in largely natural condition. Here is a place where the glories of the Lowcountry are at their peak. It is a place for sandpipers and for sand between your toes. It is a place for snakebirds, porpoises, magnificent cypress trees and waterfowl in abundance. It is a showcase for nature and a wonderful classroom of the glories and importance of wetlands for all who can be induced to come.

The ACE is also a fine example of private and public interests working together for the benefit of all. It is no surprise to find the hand of the Nature Conservancy in such an exercise, but surely this undertaking is more ambitious and complex than most. A welter of jurisdictions is involved: federal, state and four counties. Under normal circumstances this would be only slightly less difficult to pull together than a permanent Middle East peace. The success of this effort speaks to the leadership involved. It also reflects the inspiring natural majesty of the ACE itself.

As a naturalist I know that it is impossible for art to improve upon nature — that it has a beauty so fundamental it defies ornamentation. It is, however, possible to see nature with special eyes. Among contemporary nature photographers, Tom Blagden clearly has that capacity. To see the ACE through his lens is to gain a heightened sense of appreciation of this extraordinary place. The exalted aesthetic of his camera provides an entry to the ACE which is clearly without peer.

— THOMAS E. LOVEJOY
Smithsonian Institution

Fenwick Island tidal marsh,
along the South Edisto River

11

Tropical and conservation biologist Thomas E. Lovejoy is assistant secretary for external affairs of the Smithsonian Institution. Since receiving his bachelor and doctoral degrees from Yale University, Lovejoy has authored numerous articles and books. He serves on a number of boards and is the founder of Nature, *the most popular long-term series on public television.*

PREFACE

Twenty years ago I was fortunate enough to have the rare opportunity to conduct my graduate research in the area now known as the ACE Basin. It was and still is one of the largest, most pristine and most viable estuarine ecosystems in North America.

W.P. "Bill" Baldwin, wildlife biologist, recognized the critical need to conduct a scientific study of the area. Bill and I — along with Professor Sidney Johnson, my major professor at the University of Georgia — were soon hard at work within this priceless and irreplaceable 350,000-acre natural sanctuary.

The research project afforded me the chance to conduct detailed interviews with landowners and managers. In the process, I gained insight into the importance of personal commitment in achieving conservation goals — the same goals I now find at The Nature Conservancy. These people truly care about the land and have the resources to take action, especially when provided with a crystal-clear vision of a project's benefits — one that is based on scientific data. Once the commitment is made, support will follow.

Eighteen years have passed since we completed the first detailed study of the area. Thankfully, much of this fragile ecosystem has remained as it was. This is largely due to the intense personal commitment of environmentally enlightened landowners who determinedly manage their properties specifically for wildlife, timber, cattle, farming and combinations of all of these.

Once mankind asserts an influence on land,

Live oak trees, resurrection fern and Spanish moss, Willtown Bluff, Edisto River

---

it may never be restored. The ACE Basin is a noteworthy exception. It offers the rare opportunity to blend wildlife management practices, research and education, which then intertwine to protect very critical habitats within a nationally significant ecosystem.

Science cannot stand alone. Its influence comes only when fused with foresighted people. By melding scientific data with private landowners' sense of stewardship, results can usually be produced that cannot be easily matched. Success is often the result.

The Nature Conservancy has been utilizing these two elements — science and private stewardship, as well as the commitment of public agencies — for more than 40 years. We are fortunate that all of the key ingredients are present within the ACE Basin. A task force has been formed to work collectively toward the unified goal of protecting the area. Along with The Nature Conservancy, the members of the ACE Basin Task Force are the South Carolina Wildlife and Marine Resources Department, Ducks Unlimited, the U.S. Fish and Wildlife Service and private landowners. Together we have achieved measurable success by protecting over 50,000 acres since 1988.

"The ACE Basin is surely one of this country's natural jewels, not only a beautiful place but also home to a wealth of living things," according to John C. Sawhill, president and chief executive officer of The Nature Conservancy. "We're proud of the role that the Conservancy and its public and private partners have played in helping protect this treasure."

This wonderful book — *South Carolina's Wetland Wilderness: The ACE Basin* — reflects the majestic nature of the coast of South Carolina. Through the eyes of our best-known nature photographer, Tom Blagden, beauty

and serenity blend to evoke an unparalleled coastal ecosystem. The impact of this book will serve as an important catalyst in furthering the goal of preserving this remarkable area.

Where fresh water mixes with ocean, a rich web of life materializes. An interconnecting complex of rivers, creeks, swamp forests, marshes, diked waterfowl ponds and ocean currents forms the heart of this wetland ecosystem. It is home to the state's largest nesting population of bald eagles.

The ACE Basin's soft coral reefs abound with sponges, sea cucumbers, tunicates and a tremendous variety of gastropods. Each summer, loggerhead turtles return to the beautiful, unspoiled beaches of South Carolina's sea islands, where they lay their eggs and spawn a new generation.

Also found in the wetlands are atamasco lilies, coral honeysuckles and eight species of rare wild orchids. Trilliums, May apples and anemones blanket the ground beneath oak, hickory, dogwood and ash trees.

Once you have visited the ACE — in person or through these scenic photographs — and witnessed its grandeur and richness, memories of the ACE will never leave you. Allow this book to stir your mind and soul.

— PATRICK H. MORGAN
Executive Director, The Nature Conservancy of South Carolina

A native of Ware Shoals, South Carolina, Patrick Morgan is a Certified Wildlife Biologist, whose experience includes 7 years in the field of wildlife biology and 11 years in executive management. He has authored several publications including "A study of Tidelands and Impoundments Within a Three River Delta System — The South Edisto, Ashepoo and Combahee Rivers of South Carolina."

FROM STORKS TO STURGEON:
THE NATURAL PERSPECTIVE

As clear early-morning light warmed the October air, wood storks began to arrive at the pond, a small one-acre depression isolated in the marsh. The water level had receded from lack of rain, and a bounty of food trapped in the shallows awaited the storks' tactile probing. Numbering about 30 birds, they waded methodically in small groups among a larger mixed flock of white ibis and great egrets, all seeking sustenance in the fertile pond.

After feeding, the wood storks stood motionless, like archaic gargoyles, wings outspread, absorbing the sun's warmth. A large whitetail buck silently emerged from the dense rushes at the water's edge. Startled, the storks and ibis erupted into the air, departing with deep wingbeats over the marsh and out of sight. Standing alone in the water, the buck met his reflection as he stooped to drink.

This event, and the wood storks in particular, symbolizes much that is important and unique to the ACE Basin of South Carolina. Due to extensive wetland disruption and alteration, these birds are abandoning their principal historic habitats in Florida in favor of higher quality habitat: the ACE Basin, one of the largest remaining pristine wetland ecosystems on the Atlantic Coast. From many miles inland to this brackish marsh pond, these storks travel routes learned while feeding their chicks in one of three swamp rookeries. On five-foot wings they traverse great distances, foraging in diverse habitats that range from former rice fields to salt-marsh depressions.

Royal tern nesting colony, Deveaux Bank, mouth of the North Edisto River

---

As an endangered species that in South Carolina nests only in the ACE Basin, wood storks are the focus of biological monitoring. They are here and increasing because of superior habitat which, in turn, is receiving a higher level of protection and management because they are here. Their delicate life cycles are interwoven with complex natural communities forming a network of undisturbed watersheds: the great rivers of the ACE Basin.

The ACE Basin is quintessential Lowcountry. The basin region is bounded on the north by the Edisto River; on the south by the Combahee River; on the west by an irregular pattern of watersheds, uplands and highways; and on the east by Saint Helena Sound, where all the waters eventually converge.

Centered 45 miles below Charleston, the ACE Basin is a realm of rivers, principally the Ashepoo, Combahee and Edisto, from which the name *ACE* is derived. These rivers, along with secondary waterways such as the Chehaw, Coosaw and Salkehatchie, course lazily for more than 200 miles through a region of sedimentary deposits and coastal terraces left from millions of years of advancing and retreating seas. The Ashepoo, Combahee and Edisto rivers flow within seven miles of each other just before spilling into the sea at Saint Helena Sound.

The tidal dynamics of the sound permeate far inland, up the waterways, creating a collision of two hydrological energy systems — blackwater rivers and the highly fluctuating forces of a tidal estuarine environment. The result is a productive 350,000-acre ecosystem of uplands, forested bottom lands, fresh riverine waters — some of which ebb and flow with the tides — and 91,000 acres of marsh, all of which release nutrients into the

estuary and expanse of Saint Helena Sound.

Upriver, above the marsh, these more obvious aquatic environments are enveloped by a variety of extensive woodland habitats, including bottomland swamp forests, upland hardwood/pine forests and planted pine forests. The diverse habitats throughout the ACE Basin, combined with a marine subtropical climate, host a rich variety of both game and non-game wildlife, including 17 threatened or endangered species, among them the southern bald eagle, wood stork, loggerhead turtle, alligator and short-nosed sturgeon.

The three principal rivers of the ACE Basin share similar natural zones. In the upper reaches the waterways are small and sometimes indistinct, surrounded by substantial forested wetlands of mostly sweet gum, red maple, swamp and water oak, swamp tupelo, ash, and cabbage palmetto, totaling some 55,000 acres. Floodwaters are retained and pollutants absorbed, helping to maintain the excellent water quality of this unique river ecosystem. Wildlife abounds in the basin's forested wetlands, including wood ducks and 12 species of colonial wading birds. The ACE hosts some 83 species of reptiles and amphibians. Deer, bobcat, fox, squirrel, rabbit, otter and raccoon are common.

On higher ground, often between the river systems, different communities dominate. These upland habitats are composed mostly of mixed hardwood, pine and pine/hardwood stands with dominant species of live oak, sycamore, hickory, palmetto, and longleaf and loblolly pines. Abundant game animals inhabit the upland forests and are actively managed by many landowners.

Most of the plantations in the ACE Basin are along sections of river where the ocean

15

tides counter, arrest and even reverse the river's flow. It is here that a system of diked wetlands — originally built during the 1700s and 1800s to cultivate rice — provides an additional intensively managed and unique habitat that forms its own productive ecological unit.

With the rise and fall of the rivers, water levels are gravity-maintained via water control structures, or trunks. The depths and even the salinities can be adjusted to favor specific types of vegetation, aquatic life and the species that feed on them. These former rice fields contain a diversity of naturally occurring aquatic plants: cattail, loosestrife, water lily, bladderwort, soft rush, cane and sedge, as well as stands of maple, tupelo, willow and myrtle. In addition, they are managed for salt-marsh bulrush, wild millet, smartweed, redroot, and widgeon and panic grasses.

The ACE Basin's 26,000 acres of managed wetlands provide critical waterfowl migration and wintering habitat. Historically, an estimated 14 percent of the Atlantic Flyway dabbling ducks have used the ACE Basin. Together with a variety of diving ducks, geese and tundra swans, they represent one of the most diverse assemblages of waterfowl on the Atlantic Coast. With abundant food and safe refuge, many remain throughout the winter.

Most of these ducks are among the 69 bird species that frequent managed wetlands. Wading birds are also common, depending on the shallow waters for foraging. The abundance of managed wetlands in the ACE Basin helps support up to 17 rookeries of herons, egrets, wood storks and other water birds. In 1981, 11 pairs of wood storks, the United States' only true stork, first nested in the basin. Ten years later this number had soared to

Diamondback rattlesnake, Fenwick Island

Bobcat at edge of cattail marsh,
Poco Sabo Plantation, Ashepoo River

more than 650 nests and about 2,800 storks in summer residence. The wood storks' dependence on a wide range of wetland habitats from mature cypress swamps to old rice fields and tidal marsh ponds is indicative of the ecological health of the ACE Basin.

Eagles and ospreys also utilize managed wetland systems for fishing and nesting areas, especially on adjacent forested islands. Forty percent of the nesting bald eagles within South Carolina inhabit the ACE Basin, making it the most important single nesting area in the state. When counts began in 1976, only 36 eagles and 13 nests were evident. Sixteen years later, with almost 200 birds and 68 nests present statewide — more than in any other southern state except Florida — the thrill of bald eagle sightings in the ACE Basin is not unusual.

American alligators, a once-endangered species, have rebounded in the ACE Basin in numbers surpassing all other areas of the state. Throughout much of the basin their primeval presence can be experienced frequently. In the managed wetlands and adjacent river systems, they feed in shallow waters and construct nests on banks and in high marshes. Their population numbers have increased dramatically, resulting in their removal from the endangered species list. In addition to alligators, managed wetlands also are utilized by some bird species normally associated more with marine environments, such as skimmers, gulls and terns. Songbirds use the vegetated banks for nesting and roosting.

The Ashepoo, Combahee and Edisto rivers, though flowing through similar habitats, are distinctly different. The Edisto courses over 300 miles from its headwaters near Aiken, and is the nation's longest blackwater river. It drains vast stretches of woodland and swamp, carrying the greatest volume of water of the three rivers. After periods of heavy rain, floodwaters overflow the banks and inundate the woodlands with a blanket of water spreading for miles over the forest floor.

Though bordered by fewer plantations than the other rivers, the Edisto's lower stretches nourish several important properties: Willtown Bluff — one of the oldest settlements in the state and now protected by conservation easement, Hope Plantation — also under conservation easement, Grove Plantation — now part of the ACE Basin National Wildlife Refuge, and Bear Island Wildlife Management Area — an impressive 12,000-acre state reserve bounded by both the Ashepoo and Edisto rivers.

The Ashepoo, the shortest of the three ACE rivers, connects a string of large plantations: Poco Sabo, Lavington, Lightsey property, Airy Hall, Ashepoo and Fenwick Island. Smaller properties on the upper river are Dawn, Whitehouse and Bonny Doone. About 25 such private holdings throughout the ACE Basin account for the bulk of the land in the area. These properties are the very reason so little development has occurred in the ACE. More importantly, perhaps nowhere else in the country is so much private money invested in land management for wildlife and timber production, primarily for recreation and conservation purposes.

With its stands of cypresses, swamp forests, managed wetlands and side creeks, the 112-mile Combahee is considered by many to be the most spectacular of the ACE rivers. In some sections osprey nests are found in dead cypresses within sight of each other.

The Combahee's headwaters form the Salkehatchie Swamp, a remote 27,000-acre bottomland forest where numerous swamp waterways easily confuse boaters. Managed wetlands border the Combahee River for miles on either side, many are part of large plantations: Twickenham, Bluff, Cherokee, Combahee, Combahee Fields, Myrtle Grove and Bonny Hall Club, the first property to officially become part of the ACE Basin National Wildlife Refuge. Still farther downriver, the plantations continue: Nemours, Newport, Laurel Springs, Long Brow, Paul and Dalton, and Cheeha-Combahee — majestic properties, each with its own extensive history.

In the lower reaches, the rivers of the ACE Basin are fueled by countless creeks and aquatic fingers, draining 91,000 acres of tidal marsh, replete with animal life. This expanse of marsh envelops Saint Helena Sound, forming a 24,000-acre pristine estuary 11 miles across at its mouth, from Edisto Island on the northeast to Hunting Island on the southwest. A scattering of sandbanks and flats speaks for the irregular depth of the sound and fluctuates

---

Southern wild rice, Cockles Creek,
off the Combahee River

Hutchinson Island from Rock Creek, Ashepoo River

Overleaf: Willtown Bluff, Edisto River

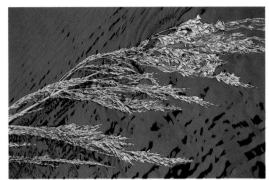

erratically in shape and size in response to the forces of current, tide, wind and storm.

One of the more stable of these islands is Deveaux Bank, an important coastal bird colony that was first recorded in the early 1920s and metamorphosed through cycles of growth and depletion. In 1974, Deveaux Bank hosted 12,000 to 15,000 royal and sandwich tern nests and 750 brown pelican nests, along with egrets, ibis and herons. It disappeared in 1980 after the impact of Hurricane David. By 1991, after reforming a mile and a half from its original location, the island again appeared and became established as a bird colony with more than 11,000 royal tern pairs, almost 1,500 pairs of sandwich terns, and 110 pelican nests. Deveaux Bank epitomizes the transitory nature of coastal real estate, yet it supports a cyclical profusion of life.

In addition to the small marsh islands punctuating an expanse of cordgrass, a few remote barrier islands dominate the coastal edge. Ancient dunes and beautiful maritime forests of live oak, loblolly and slash pines, palmetto, magnolia and cedar cover islands such as Hunting, Otter, Pine and South Hutchinson. They form an unusual upland/estuarine complex which, combined with the marsh islands of Ashe, Beet, Boulder, Big and Warren, represents a diverse collection of outer coastal plain natural communities.

The waters of Saint Helena Sound, by definition an estuary, contain constantly shifting salinities, reflecting the sound's perpetual con-

---

nectedness to the health and flow of the rivers. Some creatures, such as sea ducks, pelicans, dolphins and an infrequent whale or manatee, are unique to the marine habitat. Others, such as loggerhead turtles, cross a radically different realm when they laboriously emerge to deposit their eggs among the sand dunes of Otter, Pine, Hunting and Edisto islands.

Yet other species, particularly terns, gulls and wading birds, readily cross habitat zones, feeding wherever is most opportune. Six species of anadromous fish, including striped bass, sturgeon and shad, journey from the sound up the rivers to spawn in fresh water. Other ocean fish and shrimp, which constitute an important commercial industry, venture into the nutrient-rich marsh waters as larvae or fingerlings seeking food and refuge.

Throughout the ACE Basin at least 50 distinct natural communities have been identified, all different, yet interconnected, bound by a greater network of dynamics: the wetland ecosystem and its adjacent uplands. Waters, both fresh and salt — either separately or in combination — form the lifeblood of the ACE Basin, supporting a wealth of biological diversity without equal on the Atlantic Coast.

Moon over freshwater pond at sunset, Mary's Island Reserve

Opposite: Floating bladderwort and red maple seeds, Pon Pon Plantation, Edisto River

Alligator feeding on raccoon, Hunting Island State Park

Alligators basking, Mary's Island Reserve

Tundra swans at dawn, Poco Sabo Plantation

Opposite: Oyster beds and marsh islands at low tide, behind Hunting Island

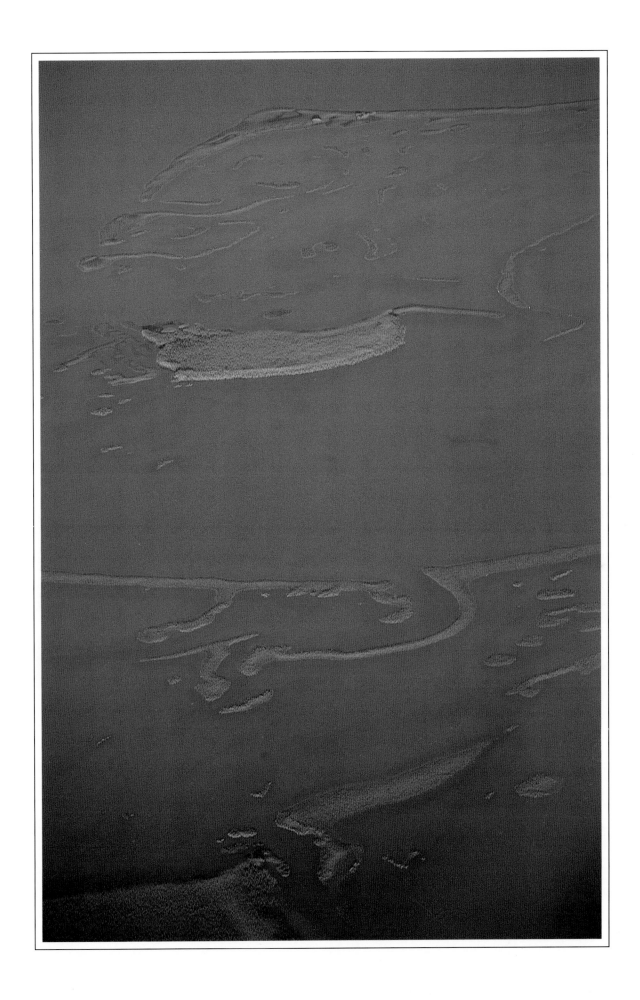

Sunrise over pond, Fenwick Island

Opposite: Wood stork in bald cypress, White Hall

Sea oats in wind at sunrise, Hunting Island State Park

Pine tree with winged sumac and autumn vegetation, Fenwick Island

Overleaf: Red-winged and other blackbirds, Mary's Island Reserve, Chehaw River

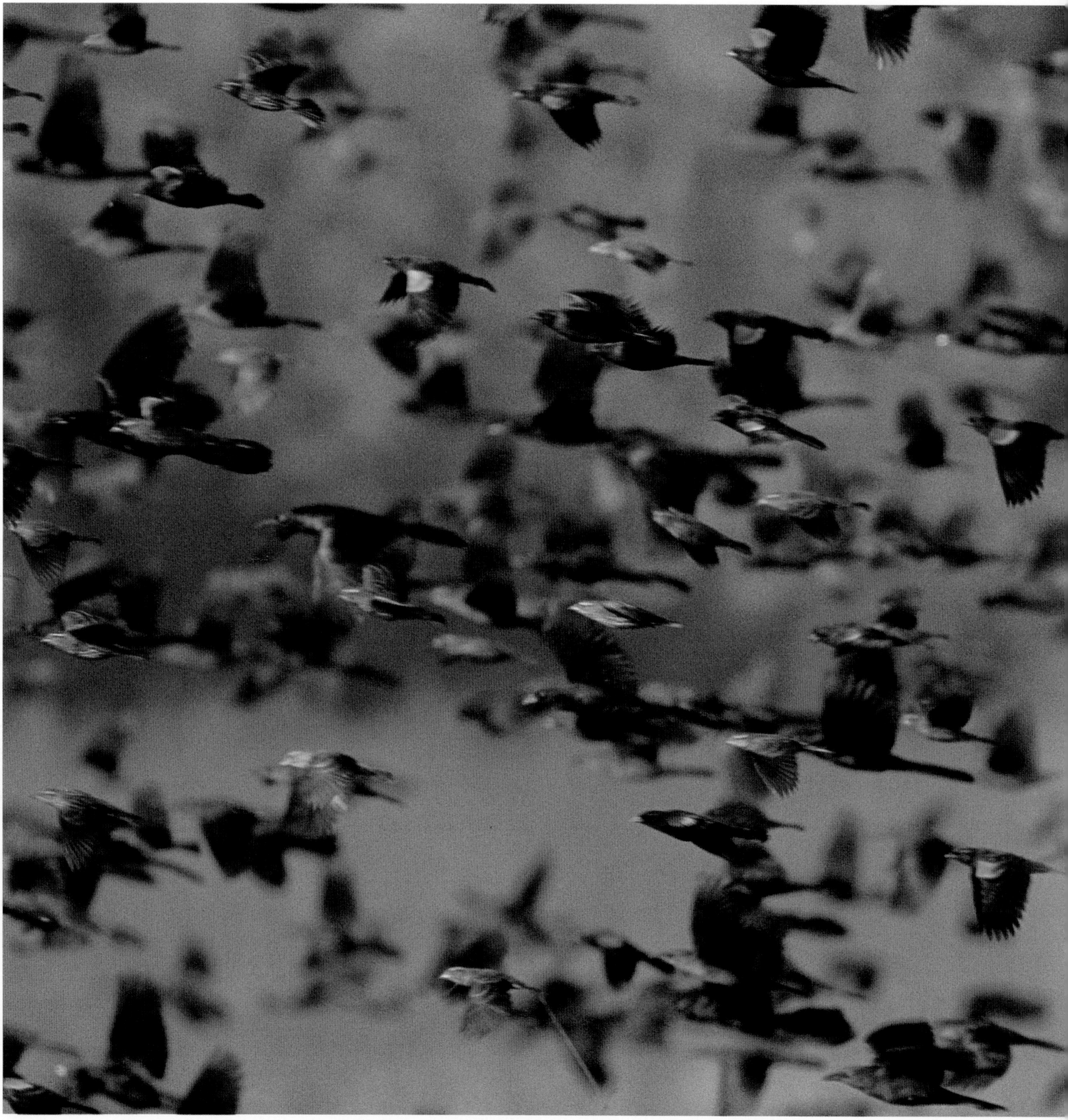

"For, if men are possessed with the spirit of the land,
so must they give to the land something of their own immortality."

— Thomas R. Waring, "Charleston: The Capital of the Plantations"

Moonrise over tidal marsh, Fenwick Island, along the Edisto River

Opposite: Russian thistle, Botany Island, North Edisto River

33

Black skimmer, Bear Island Wildlife Management Area

Nesting loggerhead turtle, Botany Island, North Edisto River

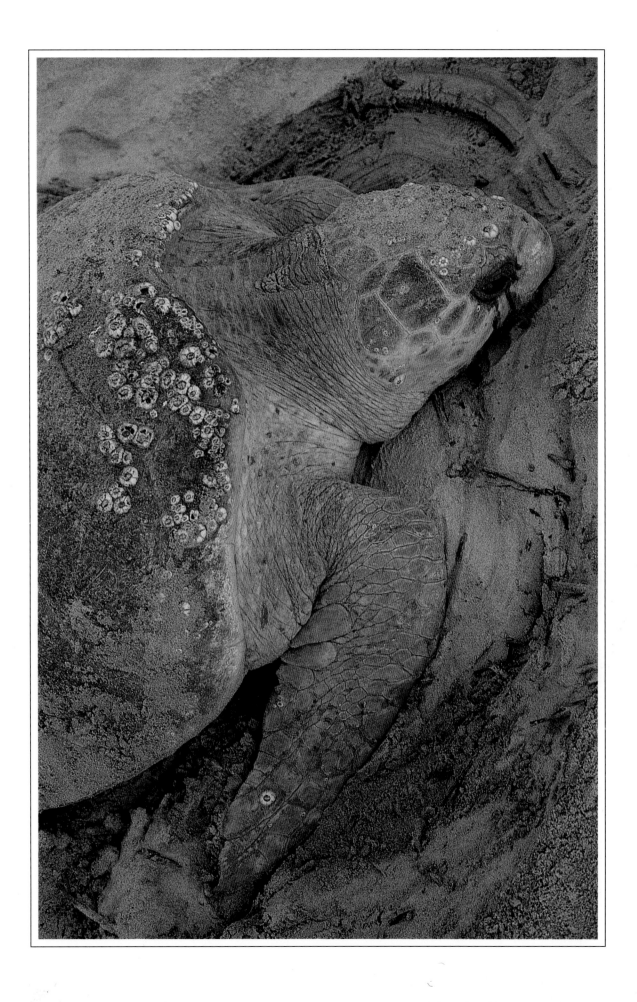

Glasswort-rimmed pond in tidal marsh, Fenwick Island, off the Edisto River

Male wood duck feathers, Cheeha-Combahee Plantation

"Attached to the retinue of every plantation home were slave hunters and
fishermen whose sole duties were to supply the owner's family
with fish and game in season. . . ."
— Archibald Rutledge, "Plantation Lights and Shadows"

Shrimp boat at sunset, mouth of the Harbor River, Saint Helena Sound

Opposite: Oak tree in surf at sunrise, Botany Bay Plantation, Edisto Island

Water lily and bald cypress pond, White Hall

Opposite: Bald cypress in autumn, Ashepoo River

FROM INDIANS TO INDUSTRY: THE HISTORICAL PERSPECTIVE

The ACE Basin evokes a powerful sense of wilderness. Yet this wilderness embodies the topographic face of history itself, for most of the basin, other than marsh, reflects man's use of the land for more than two centuries. What began as a taming of the wilderness evolved to become the managed wilderness of today's ACE Basin. The land speaks subtly of its past but has a continuity and integrity that courses its future.

Native Americans inhabited the ACE Basin as far back as B.C. 10,000. The names of the Ashepoo, Combahee and Edisto rivers derive from Indian origin, as do other area locales such as Yemassee and Kiawah. The Escamacu, Wimbee, Kussah and Stono tribes also occupied the region. These different bands existed separately and formed no collective confederation, even though many are thought to be of Muskhogean and Siouan origin. The Lowcountry was so rich in natural resources that the tribes lived simply in small groups throughout the coastal plain, subsisting equally on fishing, hunting, gathering and varied agriculture. They shared a similar pattern of life, sustained by ample surrounding land and water.

The biological richness of the area encouraged numerous autonomous tribes with little need for unification or competition. Indians, traveling primarily by canoe, followed seasonal east-west migrations, with little movement north and south until their displacement by Europeans. They utilized all the Lowcountry natural communities: ocean, barrier islands, tidal flats, swamps, fields and forests.

In summer the Indians lived along the coast, harvesting fish and shellfish and growing corn, peas and beans. In winter they journeyed up to 80 miles inland, where they subsisted on nuts, roots and game, especially deer. The land provided so well for the tribes that there was little need for a more sedentary life, and the seasonal movements prevented any one habitat from over exploitation. Famine and malnutrition were not evident due to the quantity and diversity of foods.

Despite the Indians' numbers — at one time some 50,000 along the coast — the land bears almost no sign of their presence or impact. They left only pottery fragments, arrowheads and shell middens as reminders of their existence. The ring-shaped shell mounds, surrounded by tidal marsh and now grown up with cedar and palm trees, were formed at a time when the sea level was considerably lower. Indians established settlements at these elevated sites, where they gradually accumulated refuse, especially oyster shells, that ultimately formed the middens we find today.

The Lowcountry Indians' first contact with Europeans came during the last Mississippian period in the 1500s. Fur traders using the rivers to bring out hides found them to be trusting and friendly. Eventually, those same positive traits led to their exploitation and enslavement. In 1684 the tribes, though not forced by Europeans to leave their territories, surrendered all claims to a land they had inhabited for thousands of years. By the 1760s most of the Indians were driven out, killed or decimated by smallpox and other introduced diseases. Their disappearance marked the beginning of a less harmonious, far more complex period of human use of the ACE Basin's natural wealth.

The settlement of the Lowcountry by Europeans was an inherently competitive event. The Spanish were probably the first to arrive, but shortly clashed with the English for control. After several major battles, the British won command of the coast and by the 1680s had established colonies in the Lowcountry based on agriculture and timber. With its heat, insects, swamps and endless forests, the land challenged their survival. They exported deerskins and lived off subsistence crops, game and fish. Eventually a forest-based industry evolved, centered on the production of naval stores: pitch, tar and fine lumber, which were in great demand.

During this English Colonial period a small seed from Madagascar was introduced in the latter 1600s that altered forever the course of South Carolina history. The subsequent planting of rice in the Lowcountry spawned a separate culture, a society bound to large tracts of land embracing tidal rivers . . . and bound to slavery. Each of the ACE's major rivers is lined with impressive plantations that supported a thriving tidewater rice culture at the turn of the 18th century.

From 1750 to 1850 most of the ACE Basin was under the control of a few large landowners. Each plantation operated as a separate community, some with several hundred slaves. The success of rice cultivation provided wealth previously unknown to the area. A distinct society evolved in which the planters were the dominant social class, an agrarian aristocracy. They formed a plantation economy around which the towns arose to handle products and service needs. Life became rooted to this rural order.

43

Blue iris in swamp, Cherokee Plantation

The success of the rice culture firmly established a pattern of land use in the ACE Basin which, by historical good fortune, still prevails today. The planters developed an elaborate system of dikes, canals and fields, all linked to riverine tidal freshwater zones. The rice fields, many of them cleared from cypress and tupelo swamps, represent a feat of engineering and a powerful testament to the achievements of slave labor. The plantation owners became true pioneers of land and water management. Today, the large properties, lack of roads, extensive forests, unobstructed rivers and old rice fields, all managed for game, timber and agriculture, account for the near-pristine, undeveloped character of the ACE Basin.

By the mid-1800s up to 150,000 acres of the Lowcountry was planted in rice. Cultivation of indigo and cotton existed to a lesser extent, with indigo declining after the American Revolution and cotton peaking in the early 1800s. Such produce was transported by ferry and barge along the waterways, mostly to Charleston. During the Civil War as many as 5,000 Confederate troops were present in the ACE Basin to defend the rivers and plantation commerce. In a few sites along the banks, remnants of Revolutionary War earthworks and Civil War camps, which protected the rivers from British and Yankee intrusion, can still be found.

Clamshell and beach grasses, Otter Island, Saint Helena Sound

Least bittern, Cheeha-Combahee Plantation

The Civil War eroded the economic and physical stability of the region. The plantation system never fully recovered. The loss of slaves, combined with a series of damaging hurricanes, a growing timber industry that attracted the labor force, and the ultimate competition from rice production in Louisiana, Texas and Arkansas, caused the collapse of the era of great plantation societies. Many of the former rice fields in the ACE Basin subsequently lay fallow and, lacking dike maintenance, reverted to tidal marshes.

Fortunately, before the water management systems of dikes and canals totally decayed, an important transition occurred. Already having a reputation for plentiful game and wild beauty, the plantations of the ACE Basin attracted wealthy industrialists from the north who purchased many of them in the late 1800s and early 1900s as private hunting retreats. These new owners financed the restoration of the old rice fields and water control systems, primarily to lure waterfowl. They established the general pattern of land management, though for different purposes, which continues to this day.

More importantly, plantation owners in pursuit of gentlemanly sports perpetuated not only the natural character of the ACE Basin, but fostered a strong local land ethic. Their values are still embraced by most of today's property owners. They generated a sense of stewardship, which, even though it may not promote passive wilderness for its own sake, does sustain important biological systems.

This sense of value and tradition toward the land and its wildlife is the very reason the ACE Basin remains one of the largest undeveloped wetland complexes on the Atlantic Coast. In contrast, much of the South Carolina coast — Kiawah, Seabrook and Hilton Head — blatantly reveals the impact of an intensive development industry. The ACE Basin has been spared, but the pressure is there and increasing. Historical circumstances and serendipity brought us this far, and now a dynamic and creative initiative to preserve the ACE Basin is both well-timed and gaining momentum. Its success will ensure that the only appropriate industries in the basin will be those utilizing the sustained yield of its land and waters through sensitive management practices.

Sunrise on the Ashepoo River, Bear Island Wildlife Management Area

46

Dawn fog on cypress pond, White Hall

Thunderstorm over Cockles Creek, off the Combahee River

Opposite: Gerardia among sand dunes and maritime forest, Botany Island, North Edisto River

" . . . a certain fragrance of human memories and traditions is mingled
with the fragrance of the magnolias and the jessamines. There is
a sweetness over the land that comes not only from
the flowers and the green leaves of the trees."

— Herbert Ravenel Sass, "The Low-Country"

Spider lilies, Cockles Creek, off the Combahee River

Opposite: Great egret fishing, Bear Island Wildlife Management Area

52

Palm and pine forest at edge of lagoon, Hunting Island State Park

Opposite: Palmetto frond with marsh pennywort among sand dunes, Botany Island, North Edisto River

Chinese tallow leaves and reflections, Cherokee Plantation

Opposite: Sweet gum, Chinese tallow and other vegetation, along the Ashepoo River

Tickseed sunflower, Ashepoo River
Opposite: Resurrection fern and ivy on live oak tree, Cockfield Plantation
Overleaf: Tidal marsh, lower Ashepoo and Combahee rivers

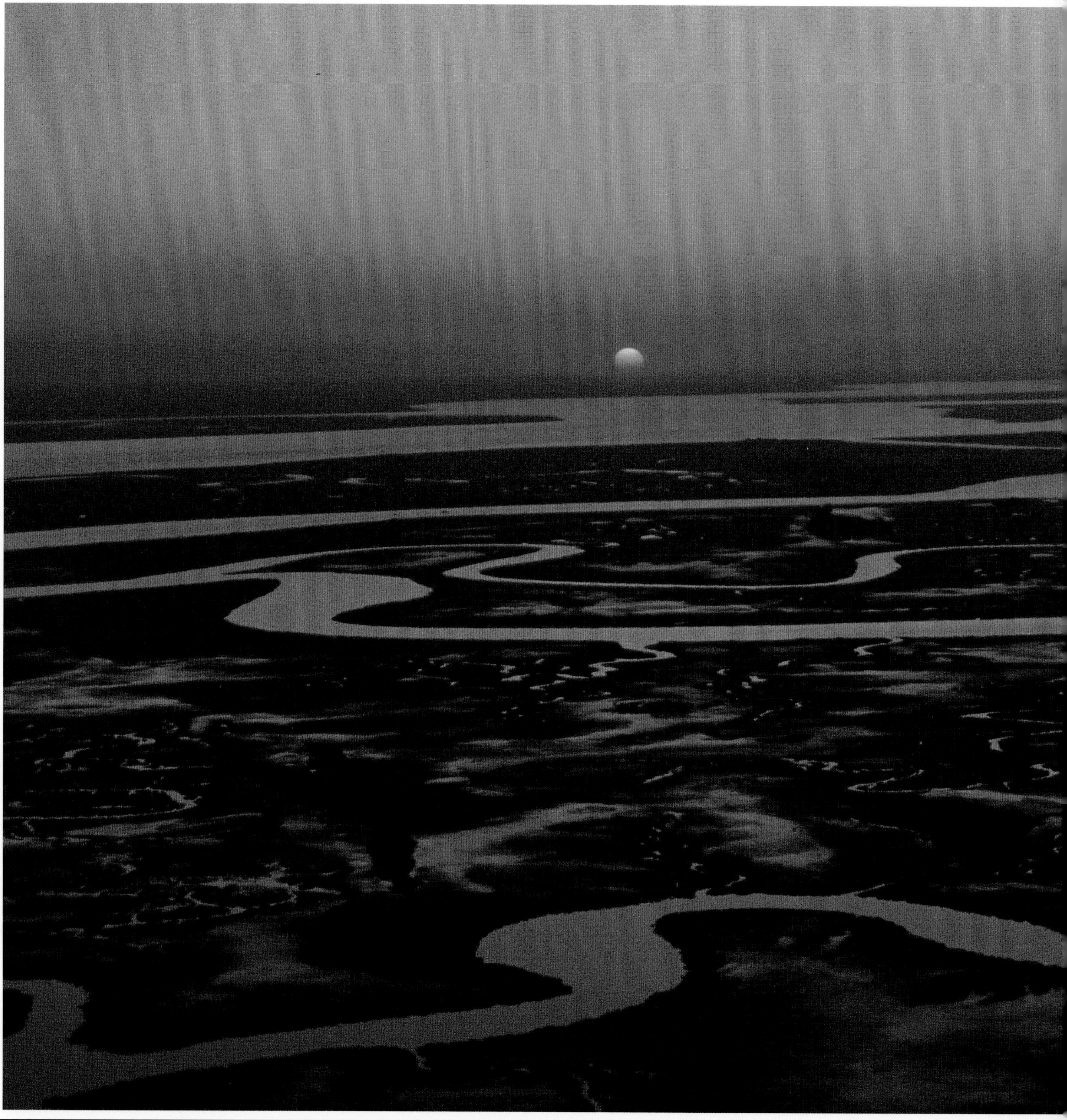

"There is a sudden surging sound of wings powerfully
beating the air. . . . Up and up they go, mounting higher and higher
in wide circles, their long necks and long legs outstretched, their
wide, white, black-edged pinions shining in the sun."
— Herbert Ravenel Sass, "The Low-Country"

Egrets and ibis feeding in marsh, Bear Island Wildlife Management Area

Opposite: Brown pelicans over coastal sandbar, Saint Helena Sound

Abandoned boat on marsh island, near Jehossee Island, Edisto River

Opposite: Pickerelweed and obedient plant, Edisto River

FROM PURPOSE TO PARTNERSHIP:
THE PROTECTION PERSPECTIVE

The ACE Basin and the need to protect it symbolize a bold, important endeavor. The means by which this may be accomplished are highly complex and variable due to the mosaic of diverse biological habitats and extensive private landholdings found in the region. In 1988 an innovative partnership was formed among private landowners, conservation organizations, and state and federal agencies with representatives of each serving on the ACE Basin Task Force. As a result of this unique coalition's success at applying the special expertise of each member, the ACE Basin has become a project of national significance and a top priority of those involved: The Nature Conservancy (TNC) and Ducks Unlimited (DU) in the private conservation sector, South Carolina Wildlife and Marine Resources Department (SCWMRD) on behalf of the state, U.S. Fish & Wildlife Service (USFWS) on behalf of the federal government, and representatives of the private landowners.

Were it not for a few plantation owners who initiated a land protection effort as a result of their own convictions and love for the area, there probably would be no ACE Basin Task Force and conservation movement today. Some have set precedents which, it is hoped, others will be inspired to follow. Ashepoo Plantation owners Gaylord and Dorothy Donnelley have led the effort, serving as catalysts in initiating a conservation strategy for the ACE and donating a key group of islands to help establish a National Estuarine Research Reserve. In addition, owners Ted Turner, Hugh Lane, Sr., and a group of partners

Live oak trees, Jehossee Island, Edisto River

have placed conservation easements on Hope, Willtown Bluff and Cheeha-Combahee plantations respectively, thus preventing any future industrial, commercial or multi-residential development on the properties.

The consensus of private landowners is the overriding desire to perpetuate the quality of habitats within the ACE Basin, quality they have not only maintained but helped to create, wherein the area is managed to sustain a healthy diversity of natural systems and wildlife. The result is an intensely managed wetland wilderness that includes traditional uses such as hunting, forestry, agriculture, and recreational and commercial fishing, along with more passive nature appreciation.

Other private and public agencies involved embrace these historic values and traditions, seeking to preserve the ACE Basin so as to respect both human and natural history. The task force's objective is to maintain and enhance the natural character of the basin by applying a broad spectrum of progressive management and land preservation techniques.

Specifically, the goals are to create a matrix of protected areas: an expansion of the Bear Island Wildlife Management Area, the original core conservation unit of the ACE; the establishment of Saint Helena Sound and adjacent marsh and islands as a National Estuarine Research Reserve; the ACE Basin National Wildlife Refuge, including both Combahee and Edisto river units; significant private conservation reserves via easements; wild and scenic river designation for the Edisto and Combahee rivers; and state heritage trust status for exceptional biological communities.

These myriad techniques place the ACE Basin project in the vanguard of land protection efforts. Because so much land remains in

private ownership, conservation easements emerge as critical tools by which landowners may voluntarily prevent their properties from future development via permanent deed restrictions. In addition to easements, the primary mechanisms of land protection are donation, fee-simple acquisition from sellers, and conservation land brokerage involving purchase and resale with added easements.

The initial conservation achievements in the ACE Basin are the result of each organization and agency doing exactly what it does best. The coalition operates without an overriding governing authority. Instead, it has a more flexible approach wherein individual organizations apply their expertise within a context of mutual cooperation. The task force, thus, serves to set general objectives and acts as an information exchange center.

The plantation owners manage their land for wildlife, timber and esthetics, working closely with consultants and the other ACE partners. Private landowners who want to legally protect the long-term integrity of their land can work with the ACE partners to develop conservation easements. As a result, their generosity and compassion for the ACE Basin becomes a priceless gift to future generations. An exceptional few donate some of their property directly to one of the private ACE Basin partner organizations — The Nature Conservancy or Ducks Unlimited.

The Nature Conservancy has accepted easements on two significant plantations, Hope and Willtown Bluff, as well as gifts of property in the ACE Basin. Two islands that are to be incorporated by the National Estuarine Research Reserve were donated to the Conservancy by Gaylord and Dorothy Donnelley. Two others, Ashe and Beet, were purchased

65

by the organization.

The Nature Conservancy serves a critical role with funding and loans for the acquisition of large land tracts in the basin. These include monies to Ducks Unlimited for acquisition of Mary's Island Reserve and the purchase of Bonny Hall and Grove Plantation wetlands on behalf of the U.S. Fish and Wildlife Service for the ACE Basin National Wildlife Refuge.

The Conservancy, which traditionally bases policy on science and habitat research, actively conducts biological inventories within the ACE Basin, providing the ACE Basin partners and others with baseline data identifying and locating rare or endangered natural communities. The Conservancy's investigations have confirmed the ACE Basin region to be an ecosystem of national significance and, as an outstanding wetland wilderness, one of the organization's top protection priorities.

Ducks Unlimited also considers the basin a top priority in its continentwide campaign to identify and protect major North American wetland habitats. Through its Wetlands America Trust program, Ducks Unlimited is actively involved in conservation land acquisition and easements.

The group purchased Mary's Island Plantation, on the headwaters of the Chehaw River, where it is establishing a wetland and waterfowl research and education center. On Cheeha-Combahee Plantation, adjacent to Mary's Island, DU holds a conservation easement which, combined with Mary's Island, protects more than 21,000 acres in an impressive wetland/upland complex rich in wildlife

and natural habitats. These two areas will serve research and demonstrate wetland management and private stewardship.

The North American Waterfowl Management Plan (NAWMP), an international initiative between the United States and Canada which DU partially helped develop and fund in 1986, heralds the ACE Basin as one of its flagship projects on the Atlantic Coast. The plan's main objective is to assure the survival of vital wetlands supporting waterfowl — six million acres total in the United States and Canada — through joint venture partnerships. Its goal in the ACE Basin is to protect a minimum of 90,000 acres. The NAWMP is the largest program of its kind in the world.

In 1990 the U.S. Fish and Wildlife Service began establishment of the ACE Basin National Wildlife Refuge with the acquisition, via assistance from The Nature Conservancy, of more than 800 acres of managed wetlands on the Combahee River and an additional 1,955 acres on the Edisto, where an interpretive visitors' center will be constructed at historic Grove Plantation. The refuge may eventually total up to 18,000 acres in several different areas along the Combahee and Edisto rivers. The USFWS's efforts in the ACE are also part of the wetland conservation goals presented in the NAWMP above and contribute significantly toward preserving bottomland hardwoods and managed wetlands.

Perhaps the most ambitious long-term plan for the ACE Basin involves the creation of a

Tidal marsh with fallen branch, Combahee River, Cheeha-Combahee Plantation

Loggerhead turtle hatchling and cockle shell, Botany Bay Plantation

National Estuarine Research Reserve (NERR). The overall NERR system is an attempt to protect 27 representative biogeographic regions of our nation's coast to serve as field laboratories for research, education and scientific monitoring. The ACE Basin, with its marshes, maritime forests, estuarine rivers, and marsh and barrier islands, eminently qualifies.

In order to protect the completeness of Saint Helena Sound and adjacent wetlands, the ACE Basin NERR project area is large: more than 135,000 acres of wetland, open water and uplands. In accordance with the rest of the basin region, acquisition will be via donation, easements and fee simple purchase from willing sellers. The result, ideally, may include a core area of 16,000 acres composed of eight islands and associated marsh. This core zone is vital to a healthy, biologically viable estuary and provides a stable environment for controlled research, which will not impact or alter the natural processes. The remaining NERR area is "buffer zone." Landowners within the projected buffer zone will be encouraged in their stewardship of wetlands, although no land is expected to be acquired.

While NERR is a federal designation under the National Oceanographic and Atmospheric Administration (NOAA), the ACE Basin program represents a cooperative effort with the South Carolina Wildlife and Marine Resources Department and the South Carolina Coastal Council. While protecting the character of the

lower ACE Basin, the NERR program, as well as policy throughout the basin, will allow compatible traditional uses of the area, such as hunting, trapping, and recreational and commercial fishing. NERR headquarters and a visitors' center will be located at the Bear Island Wildlife Management Area.

Bear Island consists of 12,000 acres of former rice fields, tidal marshes and upland islands including one-fifth of the entire Basin's managed wetlands. Numerous small islands connected by dikes punctuate the landscape, bounded by the Ashepoo River to the west and the Edisto River to the east. Controlled recreational fishing and hunting provide important sources of revenue for the basin area and give sportsmen and nature visitors opportunities to appreciate Bear Island.

The ACE Basin protection effort has progressed farther and faster than anyone imagined since the first designation of Bear Island Wildlife Management Area. Its success and ensuing momentum are a tribute to the vision and effectiveness of a dedicated group of individuals and organizations. The ACE Basin Task Force sets a standard for other similar protection efforts to emulate. Only by such future cooperative ventures may we hope to preserve the integrity, esthetics, history and biological richness of entire ecosystems.

Whitetail deer and palmettos, Hunting Island State Park

Bald cypress in swamp pond at sunset,
White Hall

High tide on marsh, Hunting Island State Park

Opposite: Wood storks with chicks in bald cypress tree, White Hall

Dawn fog, Fenwick Island

Flight of ducks against dawn sky, Mary's Island Reserve

Live oaks at sunrise, Cheeha-Combahee Plantation, along the Combahee River

Opposite: Shrimp boat catch of pompano and white shrimp, Saint Helena Sound

Green-winged teal, Jehossee Island

Opposite: Cardinal spear in pine forest, Mary's Island Reserve

Sunrise over pond, Bear Island Wildlife Management Area, off the Ashepoo River

Opposite: Cypress pond with lily pads at sunset, White Hall

Cinnamon fern and pine forest, Ashepoo Plantation
Opposite: Red maple in seed, near Jacksonboro
Overleaf: Pine forest in morning fog, Ashepoo Plantation

Osprey at nest, Cockles Creek, Combahee River

Freshwater marsh, Mary's Island Reserve

"The island beaches, where slender sea-oats fringe the dunes,
dancing to the music of the wind in the palmettos,
are no two of them alike."

— Herbert Ravenel Sass, "The Low-Country"

Dunes and palmettos on beachfront, Hunting Island State Park

Opposite: Dwarf palmettos with mixed swamp hardwoods, Mary's Island Reserve

Low-tide sunset on beachfront, Otter Island, Saint Helena Sound

FROM SUNRISE TO SEASONS:
THE VISUAL PERSPECTIVE

There are rare moments for a photographer when the experience transcends the photographic potential, when the improbable combinations become a profound event of nature at its greatest resonance and complexity. The episode may be a fleeting moment or a more contemplative experience. Whatever its pace and character, it binds with a powerful sense of place, revealing a hidden spirit.

The ACE Basin is such a place, extraordinary in its wealth of natural events. One feels here a sense of curiosity, discovery, serenity and freedom; a sense of oneness; an imperative to love this wetland wilderness.

The sun dipped below the horizon as I guided my boat up the Edisto River toward Willtown Bluff. The December air was cold and clear, so clear that the loss of direct sunlight seemed sudden and extreme, leaving landforms muted and dense under the luminous sky. Close ahead at a bend in the river a bald eagle took wing off a point of marsh. He flew low over the water, his glowing white head and tail reflecting on the river's glassy surface.

Around the corner a stand of bare trees in an open expanse of marsh was dappled in white — dozens of ibis and egrets perched at roost for the night. I looked overhead as five tundra swans flew west rhythmically in line. The afterglow reflected off their undersides a radiant salmon hue, warmly contrasting against the purple sky. Above the swans hundreds of ducks crisscrossed in scattered V-formations. The light faded until I could only hear their wingbeats. I did not consider trying to photograph; I simply watched and listened.

It had not rained in six weeks. The water level was extremely low as we pushed our canoe into the Little Salkehatchie River. For three days we paddled softly and drifted in the current past giant cypresses and oak trees, into the depths of a 26,000-acre swamp. We were at one with the water. The drought was advantageous, for all the countless braids of waterways that normally lure confused paddlers off the main channel had dried up.

At first we passed heavily logged sections where lumber companies had cut timber up to the river's edge, airlifting it out by helicopter. Eventually we were enveloped in undisturbed wetland forest and entered the true heart of the swamp. We spooked deer and listened as they galloped off unseen through the shallow waters, their splashing sounds receding in the distance. Paddling in silence, we rounded a bend and came upon four otters, one so absorbed in consuming a fish that we almost collided. The otter looked huge as he sat fully exposed on a log. I could hear his munching and smell the odor of fish in the damp November air.

Wood ducks often took flight ahead of us, moving downstream or circling back upriver. At the base of a six-foot hollow cypress stump lay a pile of white and black feathers where a hawk or owl recently had devoured an ibis. Occasionally we emerged into small lakes and saw anhingas drop into the black water from overhanging branches. An infrequent great blue heron or egret flushed from trees along the bank. During much of the second night a chorus of barred owls proclaimed their territories in the forest. By day, aside from the sporadic call of a kingfisher or pileated woodpecker, all was silent, deeply silent.

Flat-water canoeing is inherently contemplative. I found that surrendering myself to the slow pace of the current seemed to free my sense of time. Meanwhile, I remained vitally in motion to absorb all that was around me: small freshwater clams etching their journeys in the once-coastal sands; patches of clean, sandy river bottom glowing amber through the dark tannic waters where the current had swept away the autumn leaves.

I looked down on the water in order to look up — light and tree reflections danced on the surface, uniting earth and sky. In a kind of visual ecology the same waters that fed the branches above me gave back their image. They were one and the same, bound both biologically and perceptually. My relationship to the land is compelled by this connection between objects in nature and the visual context in which they occurred, all of it ultimately graced by light.

The giant cypress trees, bold and awesome, dwarfed all that was around them. They seemed to stand like individual monarchs, reigning for more than a thousand years — some with large buttress roots surrounded by a colony of cypress knees, some hollow within their base, and some with their tops broken by wind and lightning — all monolithic in presence. It took four of us linking hands to embrace them. They were worthy of it.

We could not help but think of all the efforts and publicity generated to save the ancient forests of the Pacific Northwest. The impressive oaks and bald cypresses of the Salkehatchie seem just as much a unique and diminishing ancient forest in need of protection. I hope the more enlightened lumber companies and landowners agree.

After 16 miles of river, I left the Salkehatchie Swamp with no photographs to interpret amply the impact of those three days. The colors were monotone brown and green, the light mostly lifeless. The camera frame and perspective were inadequate at conveying the scale of such monumental trees. In some respects I had failed in my mission: I had not done photographic justice to the mystery of this place. But I had no regrets. I had felt at one with the swamp. I had had the experience.

Completely alone on 4,500-acre Jehossee Island, I lay in bed in the old house, trying to imagine what it must have been like in 1850 when the island was a thriving rice plantation of 700 slaves and more than 100 buildings — an entire self-sufficient community accessible only by water off the Edisto River. The owner was William Aiken, former governor and U.S. congressman.

I had seen little to feed my imagination other than the last remaining house where I rested and several avenues of live oaks overgrown with vegetation. There were diked ponds rimmed by river and forest, filled with beautiful sedges and reeds, and full of ducks, especially blue-winged teals. That afternoon I had seen four bald eagles in the tall pines rising above one of the ponds. When they soared over the water, thousands of ducks exploded in contagious panic.

I tried to imagine the slaves clearing land, digging canals, building dikes, and planting and harvesting rice — all by hand. The plantation had had overseers, drivers, water-control tenders, blacksmiths, gardeners, even rice-bird watchers to scare away marauding seedeaters. It had also embraced a hospital, church, school, cattle, sheep, mules, oxen, pigs. . . . By 1859 Jehossee Island was the second-largest producer of rice in the country.

90

Sunset, Bear Island Wildlife Management Area

Bald cypress trees and pickerelweed,
Combahee River

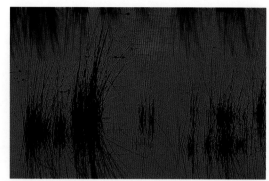

It succeeded in part because Aiken was a benevolent master with a sense of humanity and an appreciation for the land.

Jehossee Island is perhaps the oldest ACE Basin plantation owned by the same family since 1830. David Maybank, one of the heirs and current owners, introduced me to the property. A love for the land seems to be part of his heritage, a passion which helps him overcome a crippling disability from a deer hunting accident. With the help of friends, Maybank visits Jehossee as often as possible. He slides from his wheelchair into a boat for the journey out to the island. Upon arrival he is lifted to the dock in a special seat with a block and tackle from an overhead beam, then lowered onto his customized all-terrain vehicle. Once at the controls, Maybank is clearly where he wants to be and takes off for the day to explore or supervise work.

An accident such as David Maybank's has a way of paring life down to the basics of what's important and meaningful. Why are we here and what do we want from our time on earth? Life becomes precious and there is little patience for cultural arrogance. Maybank knows he is part of Jehossee Island and it part of him — historically, physically and spiritually. Being with him on the island I realized all the more why I love photography and why protecting the ACE Basin is not only possible, but necessary.

On my first visit my photography failed to render the many facets of Jehossee Island. Like the birds at sunset on the Edisto River and like the Salkehatchie Swamp, the total experience surpassed the sum of its parts.

I try not to judge a nature event in terms of its photographic success. Photography is a visual language that allows me to articulate what I am feeling. While it is the means by which I establish my sense of place, it is the intimacy of the event, unique to the moment or place, that is paramount.

We can intellectualize forever about nature, but the emotional experience is what matters. Sunrises and sunsets are a perfect example, the same every time, yet each a singularly unique incident. I am addicted to photographing sunrise and sunset because they are charged with feeling and spontaneity.

The ACE Basin is important because it allows us these experiences and the chance to reaffirm our bond with the land, and with it, our well-being as individuals and as a society. Our culture has removed itself from nature, yet we so rarely seek to overcome that loneliness by simply being alone in nature, only to discover that we are one — connected emotionally, spiritually and biologically.

The ACE Basin offers us a chance to listen to the land and let it tell us how to live. The passion in this book is driven not by love of photography, but love of landscape. In their celebration of the sacred and surreal, these photographs may not necessarily be about truth of place as much as about the truth of

how I feel about the ACE Basin. These images are gifts from the heartland. If successful, they evoke more than is apparent — suggesting the invisible, the infinite, the ephemeral.

Ultimately, I am selfish in my pursuit of photography, driven by the belief that my life is now somehow connected to the welfare of the ACE Basin. Like David Maybank on Jehossee Island, I am possessive about the ACE, not because I possess it, but because it possesses me. David Maybank and his family did not need the ACE Basin project to teach him

how to love the land. The rest of us are not all so lucky.

In an age when we seem to be moving too fast, this special place tells us to slow down and perceive what is before us with wonder and the commitment to protect it. The ACE Basin, with its history and natural diversity, allows us to realize where we came from in order to know where we are going. Not just our sense of well-being, but our very sense of survival is somehow inextricably bound to the survival of such lands as the ACE.

Here we have a land protection concept, a metaphor for a higher ecosystem morality where the whole is far greater than the sum of its parts. In its political, economic and biological complexity, we tend to see whatever we want from the ACE in our own moral terms. Somewhere in our inevitable collision of culture and nature, let us simply try to see the ACE Basin for its own sake, as a harmonious collaboration of culture and nature, supremely worthy of protection. Are we worthy of the ACE.?

Sunset along the Cheeha-Combahee bluffs, Combahee River

"Suddenly you are in the midst of a bewildering panorama of feathered life,
breath-taking in its strangeness and wild loveliness."
— Herbert Ravenel Sass, "The Low-Country"

Pelican nesting colony at sunset, Deveaux Bank, mouth of the North Edisto River

Opposite: Immature wood stork and white ibis, Fenwick Island

Winter sunset, Pon Pon Plantation, Edisto River

Tupelo and mixed hardwood swamp, Cherokee Plantation, Combahee River

Cabbage palms in maritime forest and brackish marsh pond, Ashepoo Plantation

Least bittern on nest in cattails, Cheeha-Combahee Plantation

Overleaf: White ibis, Bear Island Wildlife Management Area

Sunrise near Penny Creek, Edisto River

Opposite: Hooded pitcher plants, Cheeha-Combahee Plantation

Salt-marsh cordgrass, Harbor River, Saint Helena Sound

Sweet grass, goldenrod and oak tree, Fenwick Island

Dunlins and western sandpipers, Saint Helena Sound

Opposite: Cedar tree with goldenrod in wind, Fenwick Island, Edisto River tidal marsh

"Now rolls the turtle moon; now is the time to stroll / Looking for turtle-crawls on the pale, hard beach / Where the bare, weird bones of the sea-cedars bleach / In the bright pitting sand. . . . Each Moment a faint light dips where the white waters shoal.

Sandbars at low tide, off Hunting and Harbor islands, St. Helena Sound

The beach — the beach! Round his wet legs the water
swirling / Curls under — rasps — curls under, scuffles
the shelly sand, / Moon-washed and wave-washed, endless
the coast appears; / He races . . . with whish of wind
enormous in his ears; / The whole beach floats
adrift from the immobile land."
— Josephine Pinckney, "An Island Boy"

Beachfront stump, Botany Bay Plantation, Edisto Island

Autumn on the Edisto River, near Jacksonboro
Opposite: Bald eagle in swamp gum tree, Mary's Island Reserve
Overleaf: Cypress trees at sunset, Bluff Plantation, Combahee River

TECHNICAL INFORMATION

The photographs in this book were made with a Mamiya RZ 6x7 system, using 120 film and Sekor Z lenses of 50mm, 127mm, 180mm and 360mm. In addition, many images were made in 35mm format with Nikon F3 and F4S cameras and an assortment of Nikkor lenses from 28mm to 1,000mm. Exposures were calculated with in-camera meters on Fujichrome Professional 50, 100 and Velvia films and Kodachrome 25 film. In some cases a polarizing or slight warming filter was used. The support system consisted of a Benbo tripod with Arca Swiss ball head and quick release.

Many of the photographs were taken from canoe, motorboat or car-top platform. In every case, the scene was rendered as truthfully as possible to the experience.

Tidal creeks, marsh and beachfront, Botany Bay Plantation

**LANDSAT 5 SATELLITE IMAGE,
MARCH 13, 1987**

Clear, non-turbid water
Sediment-laden, turbid water
Wetlands
Bare soils of agricultural fields
Green Vegetation

N

North Edisto River

Bear Island

Ashepoo River

South Edisto River

Edisto Island

Combahee River

Coosaw River

Otter Island

Atlantic Ocean

Morgan Island

St. Helena Sound

SOUTH CAROLINA'S
ACE BASIN

Broad River

St. Helena Island

Harbor Island

Hunting Island

Fripp Island